The Butterfly Jar

Jeff Moss was the head writ
and has won seven Emmys
Grammy-winning records. M
Muppets Take Manhattan earned him an Academy Award
nomination. He has authored and co-authored more than a dozen
bestselling books under the *Sesame Street* name.

Chris Demarest is the author and illustrator of *The Lunatic
Adventure of Kitman and Willy*, *Not Peas for Nellie*, and *Morton
and Sidney*. He lives in New Hampshire.

THE
BUTTERFLY
JAR

Poems by *JEFF MOSS*

Illustrated by *CHRIS DEMAREST*

Piper Books

First published 1989 by Bantam Books, New York

This Piper edition published 1991 by
Pan Books Ltd, Cavaye Place, London SW10 9PG

9 8 7 6 5 4 3 2 1

'I Don't Want to Live on the Moon', 'Nasty Dan' and
'Lonesome Joan' were first written as songs for *Sesame Street*
where they appeared in a slightly different form.

'Not the Best Feeling' is based on a song called 'Mad!' which also
appeared on *Sesame Street*.

'What Molly Thinks When Her Parents Ask Her to Sing . . .'
is based on a poem called 'The Entertainer' which appeared
in the book *Free to Be . . . a Family*.

ISBN 0 330 31457 0

Printed in England by Clays Ltd, St Ives plc

THE
BUTTERFLY
JAR

For
Annie
and
Stella

THE BUTTERFLY JAR

We had a jar with a butterfly.
We opened the lid and it flew to the sky.
And there are things inside my head
Waiting to be thought or said,
Dreams and jokes and wonderings are
Locked inside, like a butterfly jar.
But then, when you are here with me,
I can open the lid and set them free.

IF I FIND A PENNY

If I find a penny
And give it to you,
That means we'll both
Have a wish come true.
A penny is like magic
Lying on the ground.
It's like picking up a wish
That's waiting to be found.

So when I find one,
I'll give you a penny.
And if we're lucky
I'll give you many.
I'll pick up your penny,
Won't let the dustman sweep it.
But if I find a pound . . .
I'll probably keep it.

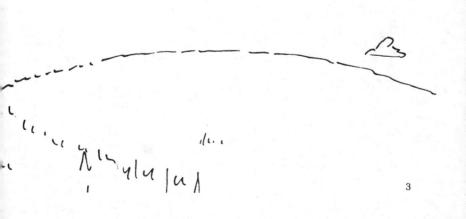

THE MONSTER

There was a time when I was small
That every night in bed
A monster used to come
And want to bite me in the head.
But I could trick him every time
As easy as could be,
I'd just crawl in and put my head
Down where my feet should be.
That so confused the monster
As he lifted up the sheet,
He would go home sad and hungry
'Cause he hated eating feet.
Yes, every night he found my toes
And that was such a bore,
He left for good
And now he doesn't
bug me anymore.

(I think he's after my sister, though.)

JELLYBEANS UP YOUR NOSE

Johnny stuck jellybeans up his nose,
That's a pretty dumb thing to do.
But the other kids said, "Hey, John's real cool.
Let's put beans up our noses, too!"
Well, a kid can't breathe with beans up his nose
'Cause they get all stuck inside.
So John and the kids, well, I hate to say it,
But they coughed and they choked and they died.

That's a pretty grim tale, I must admit,
And it may not all be true,
Still when somebody cool does something dumb
You don't have to do it, too.

So don't be one of those
With jellybeans up your nose.

EYE GLASSES

You use juice glasses to drink your juice,
They're such a perfect size.
So eye glasses must surely be
What you use to drink your eyes.

EDDIE'S BIRTHDAY PRESENT

Aunt Kay said, "Here's your present, dear.
A birthday comes but once a year."
"Wow!" thought Eddie, "Am I in luck.
I'll bet it's a pony or a big toy truck!
Or maybe a robot or a ten-speed bike
Or a Ping-Pong table that I'd really like
Or an encyclopaedia all my own
Or a chemistry set or a big trombone!
Oh, boy, am I a lucky kid!"
He tore off the paper and opened the lid
And reached inside the birthday box
And said . . .
"Thanks so much for this . . .

                              . . . pair of socks."

IF THE MOON WERE
MADE OF CHEESE

If the moon were made of cheese
I would reach into the sky
For a late-night snacking sandwich
Of ham and moon on rye.

PUNISHMENT

Eating cauliflower
For an hour.

RELATIVES
(A Poem To Say Fast When You Want To Show Off)

My father's and mother's sisters and brothers
Are called my uncles and aunts
(Except when they're called *ma tante* and *mon oncle*
Which happens if they're in France.)
Now the daughters and sons of my uncles and aunts
Are my cousins. (Confusion increases—
Since if you're my mother or if you're my Dad,
Then those cousins are nephews and nieces.)

BRONTOSAURUS

Brontosauruses of both sexes
Had incredibly long neckses,
Great huge tails and teeth quite spiny,
But their brains were teeny-tiny.
That's why the old brontosaurus
Isn't with us anymore-us.

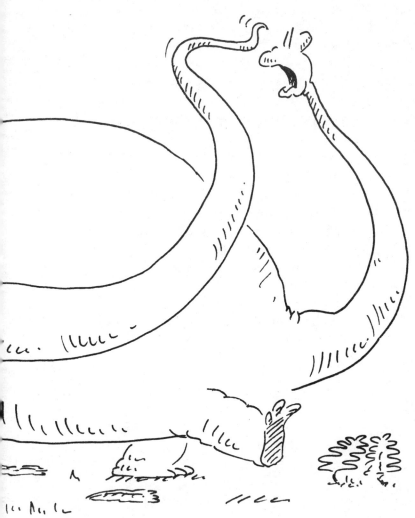

BRAVE THINGS

To be an astronaut lost in space,
To stick your head in a lion's face,
To explore the jungles of the Amazon,
And to go to sleep with no night-light on.

POSSIBLE CONFUSION

If your nose was your ear
Then you'd breathe in to hear.
If your mouth was your eye
Then you'd drool when you'd cry.
If your foot was your nose
Then you'd sneeze with your toes.

So be glad that they're not,
Otherwise you'd have a very difficult time . . .
Keeping track of what's what.

THE MIDTERM SCIENCE TEST

Wake me up at seven sharp! Be sure to do your best!
Tomorrow is the morning for the Midterm Science Test!
I *must* have time to wash and eat and time for getting dressed
Or I'll be . . .
Dirty, starved, and naked at the Midterm Science Test!

LONESOME JOAN

Let me tell you all the story
Of a girl named Lonesome Joan.
When she was three, she thought she'd try
To tie her shoe alone.
Her Mama said, "I'll show you how."
She pushed her Mum aside.
"I'll do it myself!" said Lonesome Joan
And her shoelaces stayed untied.

Joan got a little older,
Thought she'd learn to read and write.
Her teacher tried to help her,
Joan yelled, "Get out of my sight!"
So she never learned to write her name
Or even read a book.
All alone she never learned to skate
Or swim or count or cook.

Joan reached the age of eighty-three,
And hadn't changed at all.
One day out walking all alone,
She met a boy named Paul.
Paul said, "Joan, it's just ridiculous
The things that you can't do.
You're an eighty-year-old woman,
Time you learned to tie your shoe."

So Paul taught Joan to read and write
And tie her shoe and more
And Joan lived to the ripe old age
Of a hundred and sixty-four.
And you can learn a lesson
From our old friend Lonesome Joan—
When you're trying for the first time,
You don't have to try alone.

AMY AND THE CAPTAIN

My cousin Amy's only three
But this is what she said to me:
"Last night my Dad read me a book
About a man named Captain Hook.
A crocodile once bit his arm off,
Swallowed a clock that set an alarm off."

Then Amy, who is only three,
Had a question to ask of me.
She said, "I thought about that book
And wondered about Captain Hook.
What was his name all the while
Before he met the crocodile?"

Then Amy said, "I understand.
I'll bet his name was Captain Hand."

THE DREAM I HAD ONE NIGHT
WHEN I WAS MAD AT MY PARENTS

I dreamed of a room as big as a gym
There were hundreds of parents there.
And kids could trade their Mums and Dads
For a totally different pair.

I traded my Mum for Gillian's Mum
And my Dad for Christopher's Dad.
And as I started to walk away,
My parents looked very sad.

"Good-bye forever!" I said to them,
They started to cry and scream.
"Oh, please don't leave us!" they begged of me,
And I woke up from my dream.

Then Dad came in and kissed me good-night
And Mum tucked me in and I let her,
'Cause a dream about trading your parents
Can make you feel so much better.

CRUMBS IN BED!

Crumbs in bed!
Crumbs in bed!
Whenever I'm sick, I get
Crumbs in bed!

Dad's so nice
When he brings me toast
But when I'm done
What I hate most

Is
Crumbs in bed!
Crumbs in bed!
Feels so yucky with
Crumbs in bed!
They sneak in your pj's
And itch your head!
Next time I'll have
Soup instead
'Cause boy do I hate
Crumbs in bed!

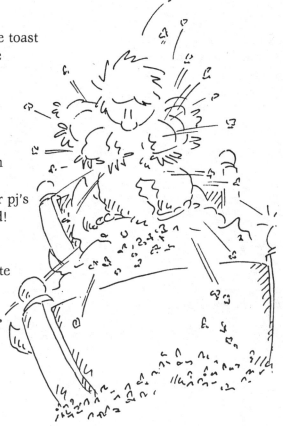

WHAT HAPPENED
THE NIGHT GRANDMA SAID,
"I'M SO HAPPY BEING HERE WITH YOU
THAT I'M AFRAID A TRAIN IS GOING
TO RUN RIGHT THROUGH THE MIDDLE
OF THE HOUSE AND
RUIN EVERYTHING."

The train didn't come
Grandma was wrong
We stayed happy
All night long

HI, HOW ARE YOU TODAY?

I'm feeling very horrible
And low and mean and mad
And dreadful and deplorable
And rotten, sick, and sad
And nasty and unbearable
And hateful, vile, and blue
But thanks a lot for asking
And please tell me . . .
How are you?

THINGS I'M NOT GOOD AT

What a shame I'm not good at making my bed
Or washing the dinner dishes.
What a pity I'm awful at broccoli-eating
And feeding my sister's fishes.
So sad I've no talent for cleaning my room,
All those jobs—it's so hard to get through them.
(If I tell you I'm no good at those kinds of things,
Maybe then you won't ask me to do them.)

THE PICTURE

My Grandpa can't hear things as well as he used to,
He wears thick glasses to help him see.
When we ride in his car, he drives very slowly.
I feel his hand shake when he walks with me.

My Dad has a box that's filled with old pictures,
In some of them Grandpa's as young as my Dad.
There's one where he's holding my Dad on his shoulders,
When I see that picture, sometimes I feel sad.

My Grandpa's not strong but he's kind and he's funny,
Still I know he'll never be younger again.
So sometimes I wish I could climb in that picture
And visit my Grandpa the way he was then.

BRUSHES

Hair brushes, tooth brushes,
Paint brushes, clothes brushes,
Scrub brushes, tub brushes,
Nobody knows brushes,

Nail brushes, shoe brushes,
Dish brushes, pot brushes,
I'm sick of brushing
With goodness knows what brushes.

Quick, buy another one!
Wonder what the rush is?
We need to buy a brush
To brush all the brushes!

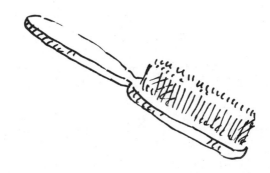

MR. BOGARDUS

My Dad's new friend, Mr. Bogardus,
Had dinner at our house last night.
My brother and I just went crazy
The minute that man took a bite.
'Cause Mr. Bogardus's manners
Are in need of some big readjusting—
He talks while he's chewing his meatballs
And the one word for that is disgusting.

Later on, in our room, we told Mother,
But she said, "Oh, boys, never mind."
"He's obnoxious!" we said, "You should tell him!"
But she said, "That wouldn't be kind."
So next time I sit down to dinner,
I know what I'm going to do.
I'll pretend that I'm Mr. Bogardus,
And I'll talk and I'll sing while I chew.

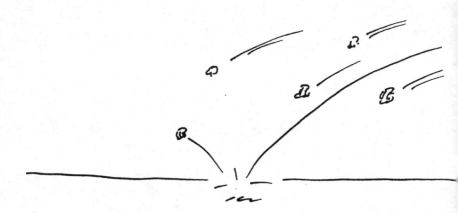

NEW CLOTHES

New shoes, new shoes!
Daisy loves shopping for new shoes!
She loves each lace and heel and toe,
She just can't wait for her feet to grow!
New shoes, new shoes!
Daisy loves shopping for new shoes!

New shirts, new shirts!
Anthony loves shopping for new shirts!
He loves each sleeve and button and cuff
And pockets and collars and all that stuff!
New shirts, new shirts!
Anthony loves shopping for new shirts!

New clothes, new clothes!
Marty *hates* shopping for new clothes!
He won't go anywhere near a store,
He'll run in the bathroom and lock the door!
He can't see any reason for going,
He wishes his body would just stop growing!
Shopping for clothes drives Marty crazy
(Not like Anthony or Daisy)
It doesn't make sense but that's how it goes
Some people love and some people hate
Going out shopping for
New clothes!

LONDON BRIDGE

London Bridge is falling down,
Falling down, falling down,
London Bridge is falling down . . .

If a bridge in *your* town was falling down,
Would you make up a sweet little song about it?
I hope not.

My fair lady.

BEDTIME

When Polly yelled, "I *won't* go to bed!"
This is what her mother said:

"I don't care if you don't go to bed!
I don't care if you turn off the light!
I don't care if you brush your teeth!
I don't care if you're up all night!
I don't care if you're tired in the morning!
I don't care if you're awake till then!
I don't care if you get your rest!
In fact, I don't care if you ever sleep again!"

Since Polly found this all quite boring,
She fell asleep and started snoring.

WHY IT WOULD BE GOOD
TO HAVE A REALLY
BIG FAMILY

If I had twelve sisters
And thirty-one brothers,
When you got me mad
I could play with the others!

OLIVER'S PARENTS IN THE MORNING

Oliver's parents are very, very strict. This is how strict they are in the morning:

1. When Oliver's radio alarm goes off, Oliver's parents say, "Oliver, turn that rock music up as loud as it will go so it wakes the whole neighbourhood! Otherwise, we will be very upset with you!"

2. At breakfast Oliver's parents say, "Oliver, you'd better make sure you spill at least *half* of those Sugar Crumblies on the floor, and don't you *dare* clean them up either!"

3. After breakfast Oliver's parents say, "Oliver, you must get dressed very, very slowly so the school bus has to honk a lot while it's waiting for you. Otherwise, you will be in deep trouble."

Oliver's parents are very, very strict. Aren't you glad they're not yours?

OLIVER'S PARENTS AT BEDTIME

Oliver's parents are very, very strict. This is how strict they are at bedtime:

1. At bedtime Oliver's parents won't let Oliver change into his pajamas until they have said, "Oliver, will you get into your pajamas!" at least six times.

2. After they tuck him in and say good-night, Oliver's parents won't let him go to sleep until each of them comes in from their bedroom to bring him a glass of water.

3. When they have company, Oliver's parents say, "Oliver, after we kiss you good-night, you may not go to sleep! You must get up quietly and sneak downstairs, to see what's happening at our party! Otherwise, you will be in deep trouble."

Oliver's parents are very, very strict. Aren't you glad they're not yours?

RACHEL

Rachel is a loud friend.
She loves singing loud.

When she plays games,
   she pretends that
She's the ringmaster or
   the steamroller or
The Pirate Captain or
   something else noisy.
She likes to bang on things,
   such as
Rubbish bins, big cardboard
   boxes, and pots.
She says someday she'll be
   one of those people
   Who drills holes
      in the pavement.

So when you want her to come over and visit you,
Sometimes your parents say, "Rachel? Hmmm...."
Then you have to say,
"She's my best friend! We'll stay in my room and be quiet!
I promise! Please ..."

Then Rachel will come over and say,
"Let's play Explosions in Outer Space!"
You have to say, "Not now, Rachel. Come on.
Today let's just read, okay?"
Rachel is a very good friend
But this shows that even good friends
Can be hard sometimes.

GRANDMA'S KISSES

They're the biggest, wet, juiciest kisses in town.
When she gets you, you think that you're going to drown.
My brother and I always argue the worst
To make sure Grandma kisses the other one first.
Oh no, here she comes! Quick, let's dodge the explosion!
Too late! What a kiss! That's no kiss, that's an ocean!

PURPLE

If purple was the only colour in the world . . .
You would read about "Snow Purple and The Seven Dwarfs".
You would sing about
    "The Purple Grass Growing All Around, All Around",
And you would drink purple juice for breakfast.
You'd write with chalk on the purpleboard,
And cross the street when the light turned purple,
And visit the President of the United States in the Purple House.
You could even write a poem that begins:

        Roses are purple, violets are purple . . .

It's a good thing there are other colours.

THE BRAIN

        Think about this:
        You use your brain to think.
        So right now, as you're thinking about your brain,
        You're thinking about the thing that thinks.
        What do you think of that?

WASHING
MY
NECK

I
have
one
thing
to
say
about
washing
my
neck—
Blecch!

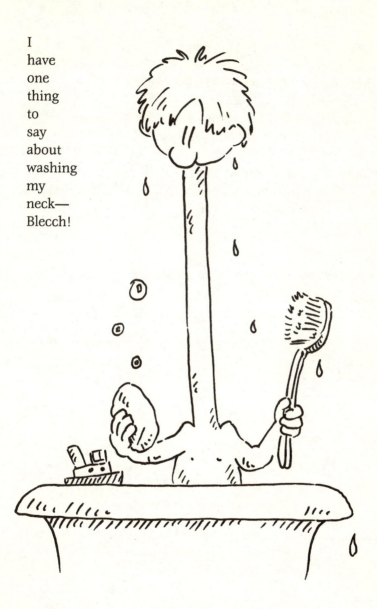

FOUR THINGS THAT AREN'T TRUE

When Rebecca says: "I'll *die* if I don't get invited to Robin's party."

When Rebecca gets invited, and she tells Mom: "I can't possibly go to Robin's. I don't have *anything* to wear."

When Rebecca says to Dad: "I'll just go and *drown myself in the bathroom* if I can't stay out till midnight."

When Rebecca says to me, just as her date is ringing the doorbell: *"If you say one single word to him, I'll sneak into your room tonight and murder you."*

ONE THING THAT IS TRUE

I'll gag if I have to eat these . . .

CARROTS!!!!

MOVING

Mum and Dad told us we're moving
To a better city
With a nicer house
And a better school
With great new friends
And even the weather will be sunnier.

What I want to know is
If everything's so great where we're moving
How come we didn't decide to live there in the first place?

SARA MESSENGER'S MOTHER

When Sara Messenger's mother died,
Sara went into her room and cried.
She locked herself in and she wouldn't eat
But when she came out, her room was all neat
With her bed all made and no books on the floor
And her dolls on the shelf and her socks in the drawer.
Her Mum had always complained of the mess.
That's why she straightened it up, I guess.
And all that night when people came,
You could tell that Sara wasn't the same.

A couple of weeks have passed since then,
And I wait for Sara to come back again
'Cause she's almost not Sara now, not the same one
Who's all laughing and goofy and jumpy and fun.
My parents say time will pass and then
She'll be the same old Sara again.
They say things happen and no one knows why
Like babies are born and old people die
But her Mum wasn't old and Sara's so sad
And that isn't fair and it makes me mad.

BUGS

A bug flew in my ear
I couldn't hear too well.
A bug flew in my nose
And then I couldn't smell.
A bug flew in my mouth
And then I couldn't talk.
A bug flew in my shoe
And then I couldn't walk.
A bug flew in my eye
And then I couldn't see.
My parents called the doctor
Oh, what was wrong with me?
The wise old doctor said,
"You don't need pills or drugs.
You're simply suffering from
A curious case of bugs!
Your head is very hot
But quick, before it's hotter,
I'll reach into my bag
And grab my big bug swatter!"
He swatted every bug
In my nose and shoe and eye
And now I'm good as new . . .
Except sometimes I get weird
Whenever bugs fly by.

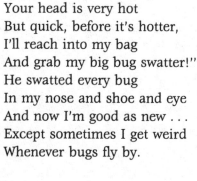

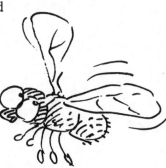

MY FLOOR IS SOMEBODY'S CEILING

My floor is somebody's ceiling
And my ceiling is somebody's floor.
So maybe my table is somebody's chair
And maybe my here is somebody's there,
And maybe my circle is somebody's square
And my window is somebody's door.
These are things I have wondered before,
But I think that I won't anymore.
No, I think that I won't anymore.

A NIGHT I HAD TROUBLE FALLING ASLEEP

I stayed over at Eliot's house.
"I've lost my pet," he said.
"So please wake me up in the middle of the night
If you find a big snake in your bed."

LAURA

Laura's new this year in school.
She acts so opposite, it seems like a rule.
If someone says yes, Laura says no.
If someone says high, Laura says low.
If you say bottom, she'll say top.
If you say go, she'll always stop.
If you say short, Laura says tall.
If you say none, she says all.
If you say beginning, Laura says end . . .
But today she asked me to be her friend.
I said maybe
But not quite yes.
Then I said, "Want to take a walk?"
And Laura said, "I guess."

THE WASHING MACHINE

There once was a boy named Eugene
Who had a strange washing machine.
Of the socks Gene would wear
It ate half of each pair
Leaving one blue, one red, and one green.

(Which must be why Eugene wears socks that don't match.)

THE CUDDLIES

"Oh, the Cuddlies! The Cuddlies!
Beware of those terrible Cuddlies!
Those kittens and bunnies and teddy bears
Give us the shivers and quivers and scares!
Lock all the doors and hurry upstairs!
Beware of the terrible Cuddlies!"

In Monsterland on a cold dark night
    When monster children are sleeping tight
        A wolf may howl in the yellow moonlight
        And no one is scared at all.

But if a kitten comes into sight
Or a furry bunny all soft and white
Then monster children scream with fright
And you can hear them call:

"Oh, the Cuddlies! The Cuddlies!
Beware of those terrible Cuddlies!
Those kittens and bunnies and teddy bears
Give us the shivers and quivers and scares!
Lock all the doors and hurry upstairs!
Beware of the terrible Cuddlies!"

IF SHOES COULD FLY

If shoes could fly,
(Oh, what a treat!)
Then we'd wear birds
Upon our feet.

RAIN

Once, when I was little, I was at the beach
And it began to rain
So hard, drops so big you could see each one falling.
I didn't have my yellow raincoat with me
Or my hat or umbrella.
I wasn't even wearing a shirt or shoes or socks,
Just my bathing suit.
The rain poured down drops so big you could feel each one
hit you.

Most people ran to keep dry,
But not me.
They yelled at me to come with them,
But I just stood there getting wetter.
I just stood there getting so wet
And laughing.

WHAT RALPH SAID AFTER HE ASKED HIS PARENTS FOR A DOG AND THEY EXPLAINED HOW HE WOULD HAVE TO FEED IT AND CLEAN UP AFTER IT AND WALK IT

Instead of a puppy
How about a guppy?

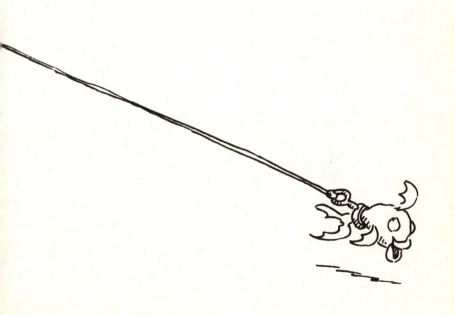

AT THE ZOO

We went to the zoo
But who looked at who?

We saw the gorilla
Looking at Willa.
We saw the yak
Staring at Jack.
We saw the cheetah
Peering at Rita.

We saw the snake
Gazing at Jake.
We saw the pony
Glancing at Tony.
We saw the lamb
Catch sight of Pam.

We saw the hippo
Watch Ms. De Filippo.
We saw the duck
Peeking at Chuck.
We saw the lion
Glaring at Ryan.
We saw the panda
Observing Amanda.
We saw the llama
Eyeing Steve's Mama.

And we saw the gnu
Smiling at you.

That's who looked at who
When we went to the zoo.

COW IN THE CITY

A cow took a trip to the city one day.
She nibbled on the pavement 'cause there wasn't any hay.
She mooed at the cars 'cause there weren't any sheep.
And at night she went to a hotel to sleep.
She got into bed and it broke with a crash,
So back to the country she ran in a flash,
And safe in her barn, mooed a long happy moo.
(If I were a cow, that's what I'd do, too.)

SWORD SWALLOWING

Sword swallowing's one nifty trick
But it's also as dumb as a brick
'Cause a sharp blade of steel
Isn't much of a meal
And the handle will make you quite sick.

(So if you have any swords around the house, try a peanut
butter and jam sandwich instead.)

WHAT YOU SHOULD TELL YOUR PARENTS TO CALM THEM DOWN WHEN THEY SAY, "HOW COULD ONE PERSON'S ROOM BE SUCH A COMPLETE MESS!?!?"

I thought my floor . . .
Was a drawer.

CLEAN SHIRT

Dad said, "Put a clean shirt on!"
I did just what he said.
I got a clean shirt from my drawer
And pulled it over my head.
So why was Dad still mad at me?
What was it that I'd done?
I'd simply put a clean shirt on . . .
On top of my dirty one.

WEDDINGS

If you go to a wedding, here's what it means,
No one wears trainers and no one wears jeans.
Just your very best new clothes are all that you wear
And everyone in your whole family is there,
Even some cousins that you've never known
And the grown-ups all say, "Oh, how much you have grown!"
So everyone's sitting in one big church room
(Except Ted and Aunt Carol, the bride and groom).
Then all of a sudden things quiet way down
And an organ starts playing and people turn 'round
And real slow my favourite aunt Carol walks in
And she's prettier now than she ever has been.
She's a bride and she's really great looking today
(When normally she just looks kind of okay).
She walks in and stands with her Dad for a while
And then Ted, her boyfriend, comes in down the aisle.
His hair is all combed and he's wearing a tie,
And right then his Mum starts to sniffle and cry.
And now it comes time for the get-married part,
The minister says that we're ready to start
So he talks and he talks about some boring things,
Then my little cousin Pete steps up holding two rings.
He gives one to the groom and one to the bride,
Then his Dad, Uncle Bill, pulls him off to the side.
Then Carol and Ted kind of look at each other
And another big sniffle comes from Ted's mother,
And Carol and Ted put on the gold rings
And they talk and they promise each other some things.
They promise that they'll love each other a lot
And help one another no matter what
And be with each other the rest of their life.

Then the minister says, "Now you're husband and wife."
Then everyone's in such a big happy mood
And you go to a party with very much food
Where you dance with some grown-ups and taste someone's wine
And then do a conga-dance in one long line
'Till Carol and Ted drive off in a car
And everyone's thinking how happy they are.
So we all yell good-bye and throw handfuls of rice.
Then the whole thing is over. Weddings are nice.

LEMONADE PITCHER
(A Cheer)

Lemonade pitcher, you're so great!
Pitch that lemonade over home plate!
Lemonade pitcher, ready, set, go!
Grab that lemonade and throw, throw, throw!
Throw it at the batter!
Throw it on the grass!
When the game is over,
Throw it in a glass!
Lemonade pitcher, sweet and cool!
Best old pitcher in the whole darn school!
Lemonade, lemonade, sis, boom, bah!
Lemonade pitcher, rah, rah, rah!

THE TREE

When Elizabeth was only three,
She and her father planted a tree,
As small a one as you've ever seen.
But now that Elizabeth's past thirteen,
The tree is as tall as the top of the door.

Her Dad says the tree will keep on growing.
She asks how tall. "There's no way of knowing,"
He says, "But you can bet it will
Reach as high as the windowsill
Of the bedroom up on the second floor."

And Lizzie says, "Someday when I'm grown
With a job or a family of my own,
I can come by and look at the tree."
And her Dad says, "Then maybe you'll think of me
And the day we planted it years before."

TWOS

Lots of things come in twos—
Ears and earmuffs, feet and shoes,
Ankles, shoulders, elbows, eyes,
Heels and shins and knees and thighs,
Gumboots, ice skates, mittens, socks,
Humps on camels, hands on clocks.
And heads on monsters also do—
Like that one . . .
Hiding right behind you!

WHO DID *THAT?*

I don't know who did it.

I don't know if my brother did it.
I don't know if the dog did it.
I don't know if some big hairy monster did it.

I don't know if a burglar snuck in and did it.
I don't know if a ghost came back to life and did it.
I don't know if some huge yucky wad of slime oozed in
through the window and did it.

All I know is
Absolutely . . .
Positively . . .
One hundred percent for sure . . .

I

DID

NOT

DO IT!!!!!

So leave me alone!

NO MATTER WHAT ANYONE SAYS ABOUT ME AND JONATHAN'S SISTER

I never kissed her.

THE BANANA KING

A king I knew got tired
Of salad, cheese, and meat
And decided that bananas
Was the only food he'd eat.

Just boiled bananas, baked bananas,
Scrambled bananas, fried,
Grilled banana burgers
With banana juice on the side.

Now the king so loved bananas
That he made a royal decree:
"My subjects, too, shall only eat
Bananas, just like me."

Mashed bananas, pickled bananas,
Hot banana stew,
Banana soup and sandwiches,
Banana pizza, too.

So the king and all his subjects
Ate bananas, nothing more,
'Till they ran out of bananas.
And then they went back to eating all the normal stuff they
ate before.

      (Which was good because with so much
           banana-eating, everybody
                was sick to their stomachs anyway.)

ROCK 'N' ROLL STAR

I dreamed I was a rock 'n' roll superstar
With a zillion fans and a long purple car.
I gave a monster concert in the gym of our school
And Peggy Rashmore thought I was awesome and cool.
She sat way up front and she led all the cheers
And boy, was she sorry she'd made fun of my ears.

ERIC

Part I: Things That Eric Knows

1) The capital of Outer Mongolia
2) How to spell eleven different kinds of dinosaurs
3) Who won the World Cup every year since 1954
4) The difference between a stalactite and a stalagmite
5) How to bake a cake

Everybody says how smart Eric is.
He is the smartest kid in the school.
Even everybody's *parents* say how smart he is!

Part II: What We Think About Eric

Do you think everybody loves Eric?
(Make a tick in the box.) ☐ Yes ☐ No
Do you think everybody hates Eric?
(Make a tick in the box.) ☐ Yes ☐ No

If you thought everybody loves Eric, you are wrong.
If you thought everybody hates him, you are also wrong.

What we think about Eric is: He's *okay.*
Not great, not cool, not ratty, and not nerdy.
What we think Eric is, is *okay.*
Some people like him, and other people think he
happens to be a little boring.

That's it about Eric.

RHODA

My friend Rhoda is always very *busy*.
She is always *moving*.
She does everything *fast*.

You can never say to Rhoda, "Hey, look at that pretty flower,"
because Rhoda has already run *past* it.

You cannot say to Rhoda, "Look at that weird puffy cloud
   that's shaped like a goldfish,"
      Because if she looked up at the sky, Rhoda wouldn't be
         able to watch where she was *running*.

Even when she washes dishes or sets the table or gets
dressed or reads a poem, Rhoda does it *fast*.

It's hard to just sit around and have a chat with her.

But if you want to have a race or double-jump rope or see how
quick you can change into your pajamas,
Rhoda is a great friend to have.

And, after all, there are other friends
to do slow things with.

THE LOCKED WARDROBE

There's a wardrobe where nobody goes.
What is lurking inside no one knows.
Like a body that's dead,
Or a weird shrunken head,
Or my mother's old high school dance clothes.

DAD AND ME

Up in his wardrobe, my Dad has a very old baseball glove
That was his when he was a kid.
In my wardrobe, I have an old blanket called Softie
That was mine when I was very little.
Dad never uses his glove anymore
And I don't use Softie.
But Dad doesn't want to throw his glove away
And I don't want to throw away my blanket either.
We just want to keep them.
If you ask us why,
We say we don't know why, we just do.

STEPHEN

Stephen couldn't read well.
Some of the kids said, "He'll probably have to leave here
And go to another school because he's such a bad reader."
Some of the kids laughed at him.

Callie said, "There's nothing funny about it.
Everybody isn't good at something.
Steffie is bad at maths,
Benjamin isn't fast."
Callie herself can't dance almost.
So a lot of us stopped making fun of Stephen.

Then, after vacation, he wasn't there anymore.
They had to send him to a different school
Because of his reading.
When we talked about it, we said it was sad.
After a while we mostly forgot about Stephen.

But I have a birthday coming soon.
I told Mum I'd invite Stephen,
And she said, "Good. I hope he'll come."

TWO AGAINST ONE

Two against one
Isn't much fun
Especially if you
Aren't part of the two.

WHAT MOLLY THINKS WHEN
HER PARENTS ASK HER TO SING
FOR COMPANY ALL THE TIME

Why do they always just tell me, "Go to it!"
Without ever asking if I *want* to do it?
I wonder if they'd think that things were so fine
If they had to sing at parties of mine!

NASTY DAN

Nasty Dan was the meanest man I ever knew,
He'd stomp and scream and be real mean the whole day through.
He frowned a bunch, ate nails for lunch, and he'd never laugh,
He'd just jump and yell and I heard tell he never took a bath.

He lived alone in a nasty home with a big iron door,
It was thirteen years since he'd washed his ears or swept the floor.
When he went outside, everyone would hide, both big and small,
And the only words he ever said were, "I don't like you at all."

Now Nasty Pearl was a nasty girl who met Dan somehow.
She said, "You're like me, rotten as can be, let's get married now."
So they went and did and had a rotten kid, and I must confess
That today they're living just as snug and cozy as could be . . .
In their nasty happiness.

NOT THE BEST FEELING

If someone socks you in the eye
And they don't even tell you why,
And then you try to climb a tree
But you fall down and hurt your knee,
And then your brother spills the glue
But your father yells at you,
You will not be feeling glad,
But you *will* be feeling . . .

. . . in the mood for door-slamming and pillow-bashing and
not seeing anybody anymore, which is the same as saying . . .

You'll be feeling . . . MAD!

MEETING STRANGERS

I don't like meeting strangers,
I don't know what to say.
I guess I'm not the kind
That people take to right away.

They act like I'm a monster,
When I'm the one who's new.
They never smile at me and say,
"Why, hi there, how are you?"

Oh, why don't strangers like me?
Is it anything I've said?
Or is it just my five large eyes
And three horns on my head?

Oh, just because I'm nine feet tall
With green fur on my face,
Why must the kids yell, "Help us!
It's a thing from outer space!"

I don't like meeting strangers,
I don't know what to say.
'Cause whenever I see strangers,
They just scream and run away.

TURNING OFF THE TAP

If you don't turn the tap off tight
When you're done in the bathroom,
You'll be wasting water.
Also, the sink might fill up
And overflow and flood the bathroom,
And then the bathroom would fill up
And overflow and flood the bedroom,
And all your clothes would get soaking wet,
And when you wore them, you'd catch a horrible cold
And have to stay home from school
And you couldn't learn anything
Or see your friends.

And after you'd missed school long enough,
All your friends would forget you
And you would be so sad and wet
You'd probably just stay in bed
Wearing your sad, wet clothes
With your sad, wet head
On your sad, wet pillow
Until you just shrivelled up and wasted away.
And nobody would care.
Except your parents
And they'd be all sad and wet
And shrivelling and wasting away, too,
Because you didn't turn the tap off.

THIS AND THAT

THIS is big compared to THIS

THIS is small compared to **THAT**

THAT makes **THIS**

Seem big and tall

But

THAT

makes

THIS

seem

very small.

FAVOURITE COLOURS

I asked Sue
She said blue.
I asked Ed
He said red.
I asked Eileen
She said green.
I asked Ray
He said grey.
I asked Jack
He said black.
I asked Lillian
She said vermilion.
I asked Dwight
He said white.
I asked Isolde
She said gold.
I asked Diane
She said tan.
I asked Othello
He said yellow.
I asked Charlotte
She said scarlet.
I asked Bruce
He said puce.
I asked Binky,
She said pink–y.
Asking your friends their favourite colour,
Sometimes it's interesting and sometimes it's duller.

TOENAILS

Toenails are one thing
There's just no good use for.
They aren't even worth
Trying to make an excuse for.
All I can think of
As I sit here and scribble
Is that some disgusting people
Occasionally use their toenails for . . .
A little nibble.
(I'm not saying who
But I'm sure it's not you.)

IN BETWEEN

My sister goes out to the movies
My brother stays home in his crib.
I'm too young to go with my sister
And too old for wearing a bib.
Too grown-up to be baby-sat for,
But too young to go baby-sit.
So if there's one age that is lousy,
I'll tell you for sure, this is it.

A LOT OF KIDS

There are a lot of kids
Living in my apartment building
And a lot of apartment buildings on my street
And a lot of streets in this city
And cities in this country
And a lot of countries in the world.
So I wonder if somewhere there's a kid I've never met
Living in some building on some street
In some city and country I'll never know—
And I wonder if that kid and I might be best friends
If we ever met.

THE ICE CREAM PAIN

Where the back of my throat meets the bottom of my brain
Comes the incredible ice cream pain.
When I swallow wrong with a bite of ice cream,
It hurts so bad that I almost scream.
It freezes so bad that I want to howl
Or drink boiling water or eat a towel.
Beware of ice cream! It could drive you insane—
With that (Oooh! Owww!) incredible ice cream pain!

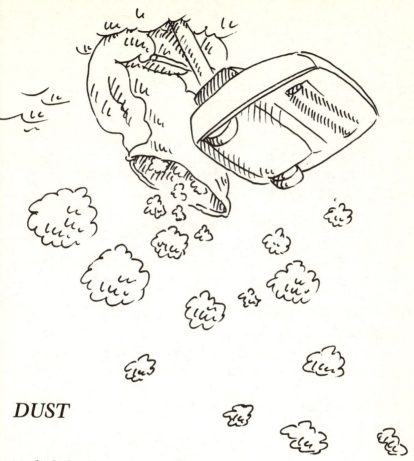

DUST

My little brother asked me:
  "Where does dust come from?"
I told him maybe God keeps emptying out
  Some big vacuum cleaner bag in the sky.

Now I have to find somebody who knows the right answer.

ABBY'S DIARY (Thursday)

Dear Diary,

Read the following and then make a tick (✓) in the
box at the bottom of the page next to the wishes you
think I hope will come true.

a) I wish when crummy Shelley says rotten things about me,
my best friend Ellen (ha! ha!) would stick up for me instead
of giggling in the corner like she did today.

b) I wish some king and queen from a faraway land would
come and claim me as their real child who had somehow
got into the hands of parents who don't know how to pay
attention to their daughter when she has a problem.

c) I wish my dumb brother, who I should never tell any secrets
to in the first place, would leave me alone and move to Mars
(where he probably comes from anyway) and take his Laser
Men toys with him and tease *them* for a change.

d) All of the above

a)☐   b)☐   c)☐   d)☐

If you ticked d, you are correct.

ABBY'S DIARY (Friday)

Dear Diary,

Read the following and make a tick (✓) in the box at the bottom next to the things you think I really feel glad about.

a) I'm really glad that today in school Ellen apologized to me and told Shelley she's not her friend.

b) I'm really glad that this morning at breakfast my parents said they were sorry they had to leave in such a hurry last night and they were happy I trusted them enough to talk to them about my problems.

c) I'm really glad my brother didn't go to live on Mars because I guess I sort of like him after all.

d) All of the above

e) All of the above except c

a)☐ b)☐ c)☐ d)☐ e)☐

If you ticked e, you are correct.

A RHYME ABOUT TIME

On some rocks
Near the docks
Once a fox
Bought some clocks
In a box
Sealed with locks
From an ox
Wearing socks.

But the ox
(Wearing socks)
Dropped the box
(Slippery rocks!)
And the shocks
And the knocks
Broke the locks
And the clocks!

(And although the fox was mad that his clocks were broken, the ox just gave him his money back and said, "Sorry, I don't have time for you anymore.")

THE MOST INTERESTING
PARTS OF THE BODY

The wrist
Is not on my list.

You can't love somebody with all your wrist.

Or run your fingers through someone's curly wrist.

Or look into someone's two big beautiful blue wrists.

The wrist
Would not be missed
If it did not exist.

(Except that your hand and arm wouldn't be connected
and *that* might cause trouble.)

WHAT DAVID GOT WHEN HE DIDN'T
GET A CHRISTMAS PRESENT

For the first day of Hannukah
He got a harmonica.

(He got presents on the other days of Hannukah too,
But since they didn't rhyme I won't tell them to you.)

SHELLS

I have one I call an angel's toenail
And one that's like a razor
From the barber shop in the old Western films.

Jeanie has one from somewhere she's been,
All curled up around itself
Like a black and white snake.

But the best one is the one we listen to.
We hold it up close to our ear,
And in it we hear the sounds of the ocean
That whisper from someplace so far away
No one could ever find it.

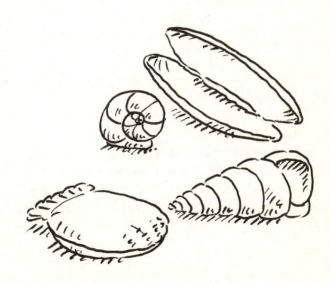

I DON'T WANT TO LIVE ON THE MOON

I'd like to visit the moon
On a rocket ship high in the air.
Yes, I'd like to visit the moon,
But I don't think I'd like to live there.
Though I'd like to look down at the earth from above,
I would miss all the places and people I love.
So although I might like it for one afternoon
I don't want to live on the moon.

I'd like to travel under the sea,
I could meet all the fish everywhere.
Yes, I'd travel under the sea,
But I don't think I'd like to live there.
I might stay for a day if I had my wish,
But there's not much to do when your friends are all fish,
And an oyster and clam aren't real family,
So I don't want to live in the sea.

I'd like to visit the jungle, hear the lion roar,
Go back in time and meet a dinosaur.
There are so many strange places I'd like to be,
But none of them permanently.

So if I should visit the moon,
I will dance on a moonbeam and then
I will make a wish on a star,
And I'll wish I was home once again.
Though I'd like to look down at the earth from above,
I would miss all the places and people I love.
So although I may go, I'll be coming home soon,
'Cause I don't want to live on the moon.

RUTH

Ruth
Had a tooth
Almost ready to come out.
Ruth tied a string to the end of her finger.
Ruth pulled the string but to tell you the truth,
As hard as she pulled, she couldn't move that tooth.

Ruth
(With her tooth
That wouldn't come out)
Then tied the string to the end of her doorknob.
Ruth slammed the door but to tell you the truth,
As hard as she slammed, she couldn't pull that tooth.

"Tooth!"
Hollered Ruth,
"You had better come out!"
Ruth tied the string to a horse in the stable.
Off ran the horse but to tell you the truth,
As fast as it ran, it didn't pull that tooth.

"Tooth!"
Cried poor Ruth,
"Why won't you come out!?
I've pulled and slammed with
    a horse and a doorknob!"
"Excuse me," the horse said,
    "but here is the truth—
You forgot to tie the *other* end
    of the string . . .

To your tooth."

THE FIRST MUSICIAN

Thousands and thousands of years ago
There must have been a cave person
Who found a hollow stick
And blew into it and
Liked the sounds it made.
So he or she took the stick home
And blew into it for the family and
The family liked the sounds, too.
So they called in the neighbours and
The neighbours also liked the sounds.
So then, each Tuesday night,
Everyone would gather around to listen—
High sounds and low sounds, soft and loud,
Fast and scary sounds, or dreamy and peaceful.
And the sounds from that cave person blowing into the
    hollow stick
Became the first music
And the cave person became
The first musician of all time.

PIGS AND PIGPENS

He uses his pigpen to draw a pig picture.
She uses her pigpen to sign her pig name.
Others write letters or stories or poems,
No two pigs use their pigpens quite the same.

MRS. MACUNDER

When Mrs. Mac*Under* was just a small kid
People noticed the very strange things that she did.
She watched the bright moon shining *under* her head
And found her lost shoe hiding *over* her bed.

Her favourite pet was a pony named Lloyd,
She was so glad to have him, she felt *under*joyed.
They went to a friend's house to stay *under*night,
Crawled *over* the covers and turned off the light.

She grew up and went sailing *under* the seas
But was swept *under*board by a very stiff breeze.
Too bad that she drowned near the white cliffs of Dover . . .
Now her story is done, and this poem is *under*.

INDEX

To Esther Newberg, Steve Rubin, Barb Cohen, Deb Futter, and Diane Shanley, thanks and more thanks for their help in the making of this book.

And to Henry Ferris, the same and more.

J.M.